BIG RAIN COMING

By Robyn Wise

Library For All Ltd.

Library For All is an Australian not for profit organisation with a mission to make knowledge accessible to all via an innovative digital library solution. Visit us at libraryforall.org

Big Rain Coming

First published 2023

Published by Library For All Ltd
Email: info@libraryforall.org
URL: libraryforall.org

Our Yarning logo design by Jason Lee, Bidjipidji Art

Original illustrations by Clarice Masajo

Big Rain Coming
Wise, Robyn
ISBN: 978-1-923063-03-7
SKU03394

BIG RAIN COMING

We respect and honour Aboriginal and Torres Strait Islander Elders past, present and future. We acknowledge the stories, traditions and living cultures of Aboriginal and Torres Strait Islander peoples on this land and commit to building a brighter future together.

The weather is hot in the far north.

We are waiting for the rain to come.

Nothing happens.

The land is dry, and plants are drooping.

The dust is blowing as we watch the clouds.

Nothing happens.

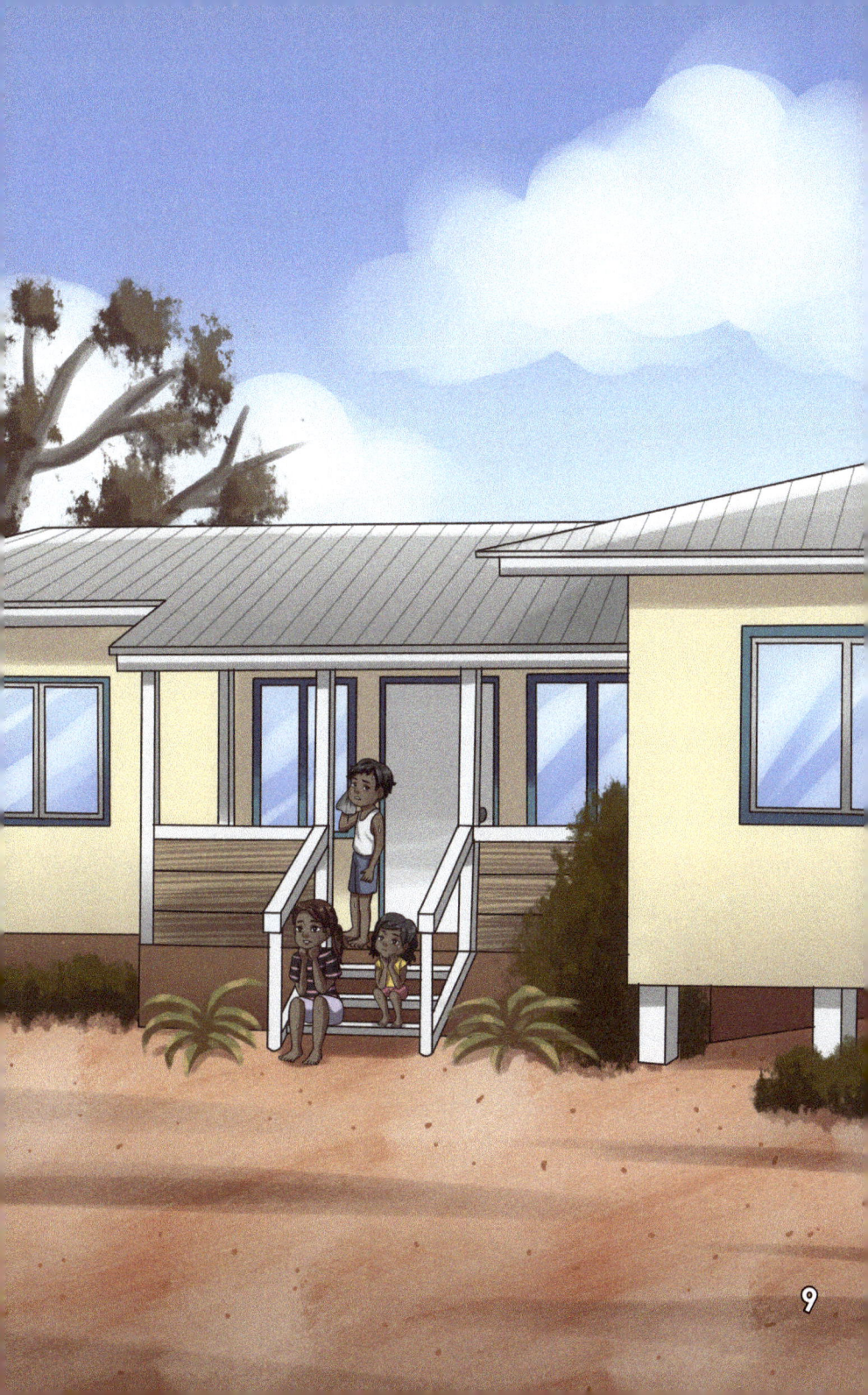

The trees are thirsty and need some water.

The clouds are gathering, but then they drift away.

Nothing happens.

Then, one day, we hear loud thunderclaps, and we jump!

The sky darkens and it is getting grey.

Then, the clouds burst open,
and it rains for days!

We go out and dance
and shout for joy as we
splash about.

All the trees and plants drink the water from the sky.

We love the big rains!

It cools us down and everything cools down.

You can use these questions to talk about this book with your family, friends and teachers.

What did you learn from this book?

Describe this book in one word. Funny? Scary? Colourful? Interesting?

How did this book make you feel when you finished reading it?

What was your favourite part of this book?

download our reader app
getlibraryforall.org

About the author

Robyn is from Mulan / Kakutja language group and lives in Derby. She loves going out on country, where she loves fishing with her grandkids and cooking kangaroo tail and damper.

Author's Country

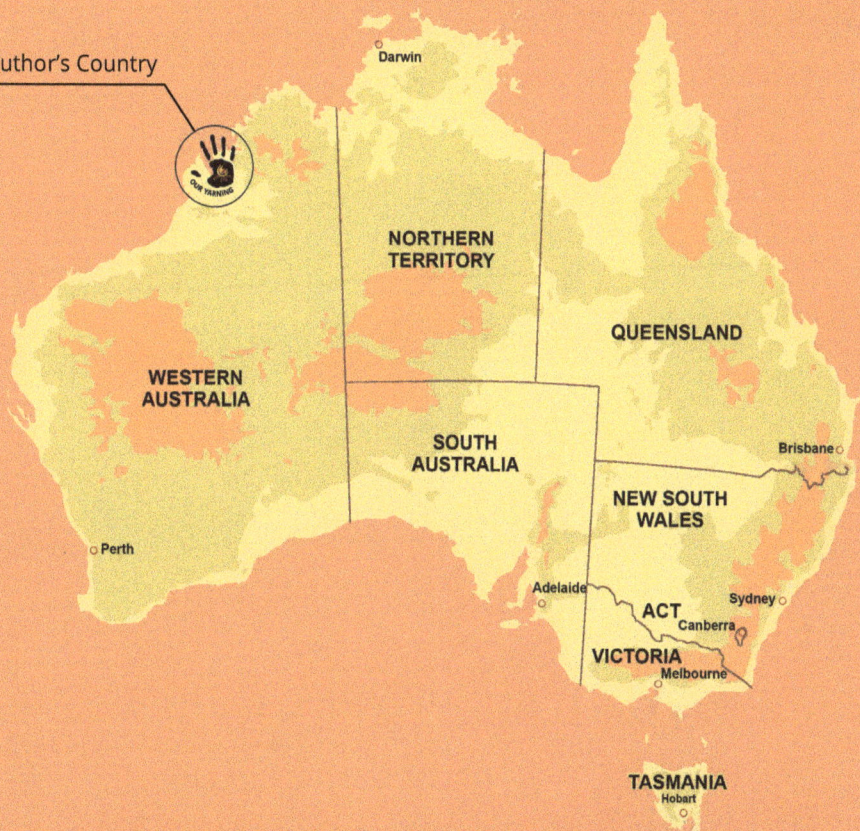

OUR YARNING

Darwin

NORTHERN
TERRITORY

QUEENSLAND

WESTERN
AUSTRALIA

SOUTH
AUSTRALIA

Brisbane

NEW SOUTH
WALES

Perth

Adelaide

ACT

Sydney

Canberra

VICTORIA

Melbourne

TASMANIA
Hobart

Our Yarning

Want to discover more books from this collection? Our Yarning is a collection of books written by Aboriginal and Torres Strait Islander peoples across Australia.

We know that children learn better, and enjoy reading more, when they see themselves in the stories, characters and illustrations of the books they read.

To download the app, visit the Google Play Store on any Android device and search 'Our Yarning'.